I0190789

The Lineage of the Arisaka

Facts and Circumstance in the History of the Arisaka Family of Rifles

by Frederic Faust

The Lineage of the Arisaka
Facts and Circumstance in the History of the Arisaka
Family if Rifles

by Frederic Faust
All rights reserved.
ISBN: 978-0-934523-32-5

editor@middle-coast-publishing.com

MIDDLE
COAST

PUBLISHING

Good Books Are Where We Find Our Dreams

Table of Contents

Arisaka Type 38

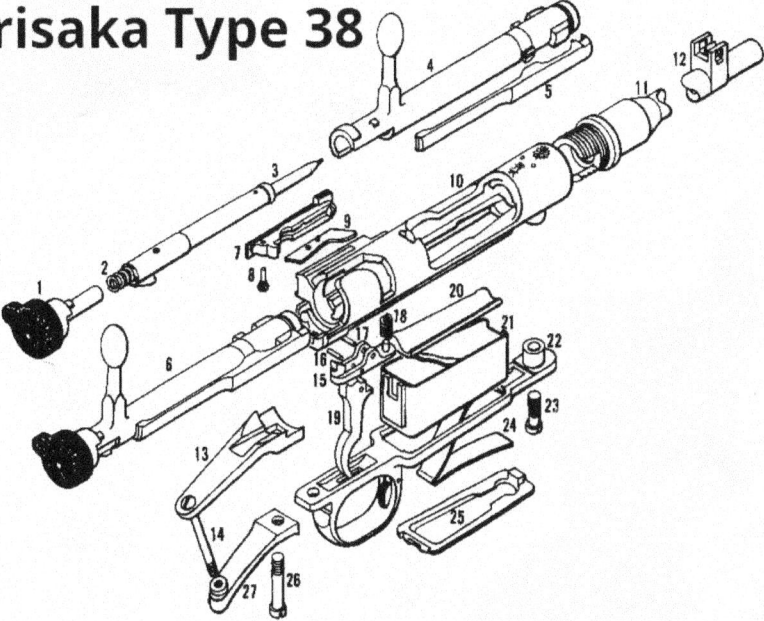

The Arisaka family of rifles .

A Brief Overview

The Imperial Japanese Arisaka family of battle rifles soldiered through several wars. The Arisaka bolt-action service rifle pulled duty with the Imperial Japanese Army and Navy. Before World War II, the British Navy and Russian Army carried Arisakas in Finland and Albania. During the Russian Revolution in 1917, Czech Legions that fought on the side of the White Russians carried Arisaka Type 30s and 38s, as well as U.S. (Remington and New England Westinghouse) Model 1891 Mosin-Nagants. During and after World War II, significant numbers of captured Arisaka rifles served on the front lines with the neighboring countries' militaries, including China, Thailand, and Cambodia.

The Arisaka rifle, one of the final refinements of the Paul Mauser design, was well-designed and updated from the earlier bolt guns of the Second World War. Its breech design provides complete case head support and increased strength. That improvement, along with a more efficient gas porting, made it more robust than the earlier 1903 Springfield and similar rifles, including a chromed bore, different steel (and more quality control during manufacture), and more efficient gas porting.

With several production runs and variants built along with an evolution in steel alloys and wooden stocks, the family of battle rifles transitioned from the 6.5mm Type 38 cartridge to the more potent 7.7mm Type 99 cartridge. The latter boasted greater stopping power and a larger bullet with additional space in its base with added room for a greater charge of tracer compound. The Arisaka paratrooper variant broke down for airborne operations into two major components.

Early issue Type 99 rifles fitted a folding wire monopod to the forestock to improve accuracy when firing from the prone position. The rear sights (airplane sights), replete with folding horizontal extensions, provided the necessary lead for firing at attacking enemy aircraft. The golden B.B. notwithstanding.

Towards the closing days of the Second World War, last-ditch models bolstered production with cost-cutting measures. For example, a smaller, quicker-to-machine cylindrical shape bolt body replaced the complicated, ovoid shape. The hand guard was deleted. A crude, fixed sight fitted. Arsenals used cheaper steel in

1

the barreled action.

When in August 1945, the Japanese Army surrendered to the Allies, the manufacture of rifles and ammunition came to a halt. Most of the Imperial Japanese Armory inventory, including Arisaka rifles and their ammunition, was dumped over the side of barges into the waters of Tokyo Harbor. No big surprise, Arisaka ammunition became rare. Meanwhile, in China, 6.5×50mmSR ammunition continued to be loaded for use in captured rifles.

The Imperial ownership seal is a 16-petal chrysanthemum appropriately known as the Chrysanthemum Flower Seal. The symbol is roll-stamped over the top of the receiver ring on all official Imperial-issue rifles. At the war's conclusion, most were defaced by filing, grinding, or stamping over.

Many Chrysanthemum seals were completely ground off, obliterated as it were. In comparison, others were scarred with a chisel strike or barely scratched off. Some defaced Arisaka rifles show the number 0 redundantly stamped around the edges of the Chrysanthemum. Having been donated to military schools or sold to other nations, these rifles were no longer the emperor's property.

There are conflicting claims about whether surrender terms of the Imperial Japanese Military mandated defacing. In sharp contrast, some historians assert under General Douglas MacArthur's orders (commander of occupation forces), the Imperial mums were ground off receiver rings. No documentation from Imperial Japanese or U.S. forces has been discovered mandating the defacing. Most Arisakas with surviving imperial chrysanthemums are in Japan, except for war trophies taken before the surrender and rifles captured by Chinese forces.

After the war ended, InterArmco and other purveyors of military surplus bolt guns imported boatloads of Lee-Enfields, M1917 Enfields, Mausers, 03 and 03A3 Springfields, and Japanese Arisakas to the United States. Noted firearms writer P.O. Ackley wondered which ones were safe for hand loads. He tested all of them. Destructive tests proved the Type 99 Arisaka action to be the most robust. In short, he tried to blow up a Type 99 Arisaka and failed!

At the Aberdeen Proving Grounds, General Julian S. Hatcher, Army Ordnance Corps, repeated the experiment and confirmed the results. His lab further revealed that Type 99 bolts and receivers were machined from an alloy similar to SAE steel grade 1085, boasting a carbon content of 0.80% to 0.90% and manganese content of 0.60% to 0.90%. Very late war, Arisaka rifles were founded upon poor-quality steel.

Hatcher's notes also point out how the Arisaka chamber more completely surrounds the cartridge within the barrel shank and boasts excellent gas venting in the event of a ruptured case. Military surplus Arisakas exported to the United States include Type 38 carbines re-barrelled and re-chambered to caliber 7.62×39mm Russian. Some Type 38 rifles captured by the Chinese Kuomintang forces were converted to fire the 7.92×57mm Mauser round.

In 1910, a minimal production run of Type 38 rifles was manufactured for export to the Republic of Mexico, proudly emblazoned with the Mexican coat of arms in place of the Imperial Chrysanthemum. Few of the rifles arrived before the Mexican Revolution. Most remained in Japan until World War I, when they sold to weapons-hungry Imperial Russia.

Before Arisaka: The Murata

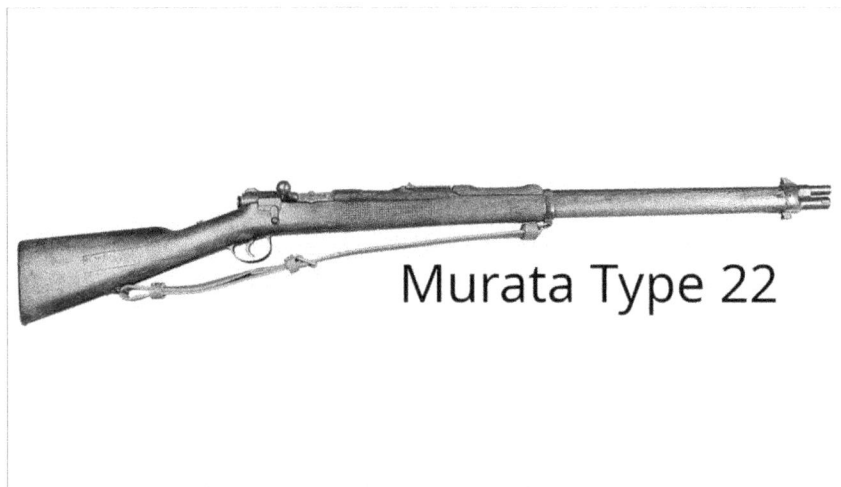

Murata Type 22

The Arisaka family of rifles and carbines was predated by the **Murata rifle** (村田銃 , Murata jū), Imperial Japan's standard infantry weapons during the First Sino-Japanese War and the Boxer Rebellion. Murata development was lengthy and involved as feudal japan built its industrial base. Up to this time, the early Imperial Japan Army had relied on imports: the Spencer repeating rifle, the French Chassepot, and the British Snider-

3

Enfield.

The Murata Type 13 (M1880) (13th Year), invented by Major Murata Tsuneyoshi, was Japan's first attempt at an indigenously designed and produced infantry rifle. A single-shot bolt action chambered the 11X60 R black powder cartridge; the weapon lacked a safety and an ejector. A flat spring powered the firing pin. Spent cases are cleared manually by tipping the rifle upright or flipping the brass out of the receiver with a finger. In 1885, a bayonet lug was added, along with other minor configurations, leading to its redesignation as Type 18.

In 1889, the addition of tubular and box magazines lent Murata an eight-round capacity. A flat nose bullet prevented accidental discharge in the tubular magazine. It was feared that a pointed nose might set off the round just ahead of it under recoil. For added protection, Murata ammunition also featured recessed primers.

Caliber was reduced from 11mm to 8x53 mm R, a black powder cartridge later updated to smokeless powder. Type 22 was Japan's first-ever military weapon to burn smokeless powder. The bullet weighs 240 grains, and the powder charge 34.6 grains. The front sight is an inverted "V" front and a ladder rear sight. Type 22s continued to serve into the 20th century as training rifles in military schools.

Finally, you may hear grumbling amongst aficionados about how missing bolt heads are ubiquitous on Meiji 22 Murata. It's true. Here's why. Once the Arisaka rifle was adopted, the Murata was re-issued for training. All the bolt heads were removed. Once declared obsolete and available for sale as military surplus and unusable due to the lack of a bolt head, most were melted down for their steel content. This is the answer to why Murata's are rarely encountered with the bolt heads.

The History and Development of Type 30

Type 30 was the first rifle in the Arisaka series. Chambered in 6.5×50mmSR, the Type 30 rifle Arisaka (year 30 type infantry firearm) box-fed bolt-action repeating rifle was the standard infantry weapon of Imperial Japan's Army from 1897 until around 1921. In December of 1895, the Imperial Japanese Army began developing a replacement for its Murata rifle used since 1880.

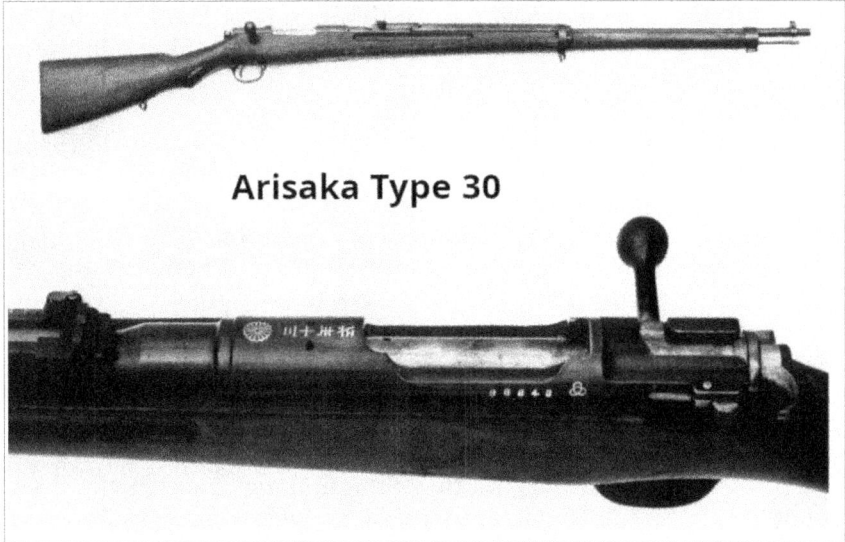

Arisaka Type 30

Colonel Arisaka Nariakira oversaw the project at the Koishikawa arsenal in Tokyo. Type 30 would become the first in a series of rifles fielded throughout World War II.

Initially, the Arisaka Type 30 fired the semi-rimmed 6.5×50mm Arisaka cartridge. The leaf adjusted up to 2,000 meters (2,200 yards) in range. Besides the standard rifle, there was also a shorter carbine variant, measuring 962 mm/37.9 inches long, and intended for the cavalry and other troops who required a shorter, lighter weapon. Its leaf adjusted to 1,500 meters (1,600 yards in range). After enhancements, the prototype designated the Type 29 rifle was further re-designated as the Type 30. In 1899 it went into production equipped with the Type 30 bayonet.

Japanese forces carried the Type 30 into combat on the front lines during the Russo-Japanese War. Even though it significantly improved the previous Type 22 rifle/Murata, it suffered reliability and safety issues. Based on experiences gained in combat, an enhanced version, the Type 38 rifle, was introduced in 1905. Not all units were issued the new version. During both World Wars, the Japanese Army retained a mix of models.

Besides Japan, the Type 30 armed numerous nations during and after World War I. The most predominant customer was the Russian Empire, which ordered up to 600,000 Arisaka rifles. At least half of them were Type 30 rifles and Carbines.

Early in World War One, Britain ordered Type 30s and Type

5

38s from Japan as a stopgap until the supply of homegrown Lee–Enfield rifles caught up with demand. Some Arisaka rifles were handed over to the Royal Navy and Arab Forces fighting alongside Lawrence of Arabia.

Most of these Type 30s and Type 38s were allocated to Russia in 1916, which was far more desperate for arms. Russia also bought thousands of Type 30, Type 35, and Type 38 rifles and carbines from Japan. Many rifles were abandoned in Finland or captured by Red Finns during the Finnish Civil War as the Soviets had armed them with Arisakas. Later, Finland gave some of these rifles to Estonia, receiving other weapons from various sources. Estonia later converted some or all to fire .303 British ammo as the U.K. had supplied Estonia with Vickers machine guns and Pattern 14 rifles. During the Russian Civil War fighting, the Czechoslovak Legion carried Japanese Arisakas, including the Type 30, as their primary battle rifle. The long rifle was the main production version. Carbine versions were for cavalry and mounted troops.

The Type 30 Carbine

The Type 30 carbine or cavalry rifle measures 300 mm/11.8 inches shorter than the infantry model. More particularly, the carbine barrel measures 480 mm/18.9 inches against 790 mm/31.1 inches for the standard infantry issue. Intended to be issued to cavalry troops with a modern carbine, it differed from the standard infantry rifle. Beyond the shorter barrel and stock is that it lacked a hand guard over the barrel, the rear sight ladder only elevated to 1,500 meters (compared to the rifle's 2,000-meter range), the front sight featured protection guards on both sides, as well as slight changes to the bolt stop latch. Sling swivels were relocated to the left-hand side of the rifle to prevent the bolt handle from digging into the cavalry trooper's back. Pre-production versions lacked a bayonet.

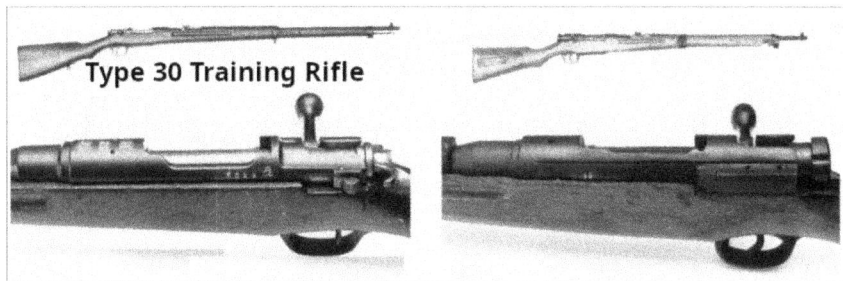
Type 30 Training Rifle

The Type 30 Training Rifle

Between 1905–1921, about 10,000 Type 30s were converted to blank-firing training rifles. The formerly rifle barrel was a reamed out to smooth bore. Receiver markings, including the Imperial Chrysanthemum, were ground off. Kanji characters stating it was a blank-firing guns were roll-stamped across the top of the receiver ring.

The Manchu Arisaka – Type C

A Manchu Arisaka is a Chinese contract-built Arisaka Type 30 rifle. The Chinese military designation remains unknown. Two versions exist, named after Chinese receiver markings on the receiver. They translate to: Kuang-Hsu 29 year made and Kuang-Hsu 31 year made. No official designations were assigned. During the late Qing China, imported weapons were not given an official designation and were referred to by their original foreign nomenclature or simply given a descriptive name. Imperial documents refer to imported Type 30s as: 6.5 mm caliber, five-shot repeating infantry rifles. Koishikawa Arsenal, the manufacturer, referred to its Chinese contract Type 30 rifles and carbines as Type C from the word China.

In 1899 Japanese Ministry of Army (Emperor Kuangthsu Year 25th) gifted the Governors-General of Liangjiang a Type 30 rifle. A couple of years later (1904), General Yuan of China's Imperial Army contracted with Mitsui-Okura to purchase Type 30 rifles and carbines. Terms of the contract stipulated that instead of

Type 30 and an Imperial Japanese Chrysanthemum, the receiver ring would be stamped Kuangtshu 29th year accompanied by an Imperial Dragon. The coiled dragon represents the reign of the Manchu Emperor, Kuang-Hsu, the nominal Emperor of China at the time. His years of reign, when the rifles were produced, were the 29th and 31st, respectively. Another requirement was replacing the original ladder rear sight with a Mauser tangent rear sight and full upper hand guard. Except for the crest, and rear sight, Manchu Arisaka rifles and carbines are almost identical to the original Type 30.

While emperor Kuang-Hsu's name appeared on the rifle, the natural person behind the contract of these rifles was Japanese General Yuan Shikai. Very little is known about Manchu Arisakas because so few of the approximately 31,000 rifles built are still known to exist. Most were severely worn rifles imported from mainland China to the United States in the 1980s.

The North China Type 30 Carbine Copy

This crudely-built copy of the Japanese Type 30 carbine was built in China to supply Japan's puppet troops. Believed to have been made in Tientsin, there is a significant difference between the Chinese and Japanese Type 30 carbine: The copycat firearm chambered in 7.92×57mm Mauser (8mm Mauser), butt stock is one-piece construction as opposed to the two-piece stock used by the Japanese. Further, a Cherry Blossom emblem marks the receiver instead of the Japanese Imperial Chrysanthemum on Japanese arms. Characters translate to North China Type 19 adorn the receiver ring. This 19-nomenclature likely means the 19th year of the Showa Era, or 1944. The proper military designation is unknown. Confusingly, another North China Type 19 is based on Type 30.

Soon after the Imperial Japanese Army adopted the Type 30, its leadership realized the need for a modern replacement for its obsolete Type 22 Murata rifles currently issued to its Special Naval Landing Forces. Furthermore, the Tokyo Artillery Arsenal had stopped manufacturing the black powder loaded 8×52.5Rmm Murata cartridge. Army Captain Kijirō Nambu of the Tokyo Artillery Arsenal was assigned to correct the inadequacies of arising on the battlefield with the Type 30.

Minor modifications intended to overcome some Type 30 defects included converting the rear sight leaf ladder from a slide-out to a fan-out (扇転式) and addition of a dust cover (遊底覆). Unlike the Type 38, the crudely-designed dust cover did not connect to the bolt action and had to be moved manually before and after firing. The modified design did not solve the shortcomings of the Type 30, and it came to pass that the Type 38 rifle superseded it.

The Manchu Arisaka

A Manchu Arisaka is a Chinese contract-built Arisaka Type 30 rifle. Collectors affectionately refer to them as Manchu Arisakas. The proper Chinese military designation for them remains unknown. Two known versions exist, named after Chinese receiver markings on the receiver. They translate to read: Kuang-Hsu 29 year made and Kuang-Hsu 31 year made.

In place of the expected Japanese Imperial, Chrysanthemum roll stamped on the receiver, we find a coiled dragon representing the reign of the Manchu Emperors. Kuang-Hsu, the nominal Emperor of China at the time. His years of reign, when the rifles were produced, were the 29th and 31st, respectively. While emperor Kuang-Hsu's name appears on the rifle, the natural person behind the contract of these rifles was Japanese General Yuan Shikai. Very little is known about Manchu Ariskas because so few of the approximately 31,000 rifles built are still known to exist. Most were severely worn rifles imported in the 1980s from mainland China to the United States.

The Type 35 Rifle

The type 35 rifle, designated as the Type 35 navy rifle, chambered in 6.5×50mmSR Type 30, was a design improvement engineered by Major Nambu Kijir. Based on the Imperial Japanese Navy Land Forces Type 30, notable changes include:

- The addition of a tangent-type rear sight.
- A separate sliding bolt cover, as opposed to simultaneously moving cover on all other types after the same kind later used on the Type 45 Siamese Mauser.
- A large knob cocking piece replaces the hook safety to protect against toxic gases in the event of a blown primer.
- A bigger bolt handle knob.
- An improved bolt head.

9

- A gas port in the bolt body.
- An improved chamber for better cartridge feeding.

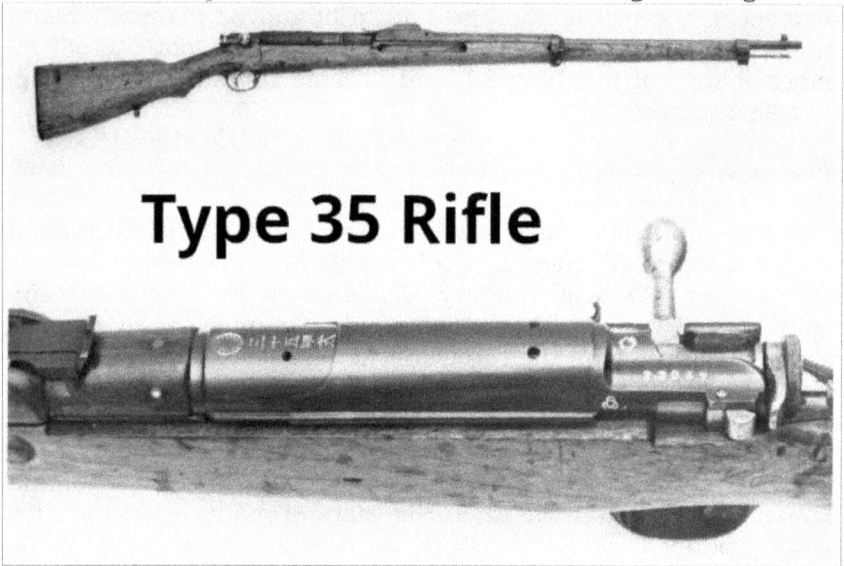

The Type 35 Rifle (三十五年式), created from the Type 30 rifle, was the Imperial Japanese Navy replacement for its aging Type 22 Murata rifles. An attempt to correct the deficiencies of the Type 30 rifle, the 35 nomenclature refers to the adoption date, Year 35 (1902), in the Meiji period of the Japanese calendar. Officially designated as the Type 35 navy rifle, was chambered in 6.5×50mmSR Type 30. This design improvement by Major Nambu Kijir, was based on Type 30 for the Imperial Japanese Navy Land Forces. Notable changes include

The 02/45 Rifle

Little is known about these rifles, including their official designation if it ever had one. Collectors affectionately refer to them as 02, as in the year 1902 when the Type 35s were adopted. And alternatively as 45, as in 1945 when the rifles were allegedly built. The maker was thought to be the Izawa Firearms Manufactory in Osaka, but not confirmed. That is why the company was extensively involved in making training rifles and machine guns of that type and likely had parts lying around used for making 02/40 rifles.

Pre-production Type 35 Hiroki Sub-caliber Training Device barreled actions, and uncompleted rifles were mated with Type 99 long rifle trainer stocks and a catch-all of odd parts to cobble together functional rifles for the ever-desperate Japanese war effort. Most lack serial numbers and dust covers. Some barrels used in the assembly of these rifles show reject stamps, and some Type 35 receiver markings suggest they were scrapped or decommissioned. After burning through all the Type 35, 38, and 30 barrels on hand, makers resorted to installing training machine gun barrels. Some of these rifles reportedly were issued during the invasion of Okinawa.

The Type 38 Rifle

The title Type 38 derives from the fact it was adopted in the 38th year of the reign of the Meiji Emperor. A Model 1898 Mauser variant employs front-locking lugs, a positive one-piece collar-mounted extractor, and a five-round box magazine replete with a removable floor plate and excess gas release effected by the enclosed bolt rear. Unlike the Mauser, the Arisaka bolt cocks on closing, facilitating rapid manipulation of the bolt and easier extraction of the spent cartridge.

When the Imperial Japanese Army unveiled the Type 30 rifle in 1897, the weapon suffered numerous shortcomings, highlighted in combat during the Russo-Japanese War. Maladies included bursting cartridges, a poorly designed lock that allowed excess gunpowder to accumulate, burning the shooter's face, frequent failures to fire, jammed loading, difficulty cleaning, and failures to reliably extract cartridges.

Major Kijiro Nambu took on the task of redesigning the Type 30 rifle, introduced in 1906. He reduced the number of Type 30 bolt parts from nine to six. He simplified the bolt's manufacture and made it, so no tools were necessary for disassembly. Due to lessons learned during the Russo-Japanese War, when dust often rendered rifles inoperable, Nambu added a dust cover.

Type 30 rifles were assembled in several locations in China and Japan:
- Tokyo Arsenal, Japan, from 1906 to 1932; 2,029,000 units are estimated to have been built.
- Kokura arsenal, from 1933 until 1941: 494,700 units, is estimated to have been built.
- Nagoya, Japan, arsenal, from 1932 to 1942: 312,500

11

units, estimated to have been built.
• Jinsen, now known as Incheon arsenal, from 1942 until 1942: 13,400 units, estimated to have been built.
• Hoten, formerly called Mukden arsenal, before the Japanese took over operations, now known as Shenyang arsenal, from 1937 until 1944: 148,800 units, estimated to have been built.

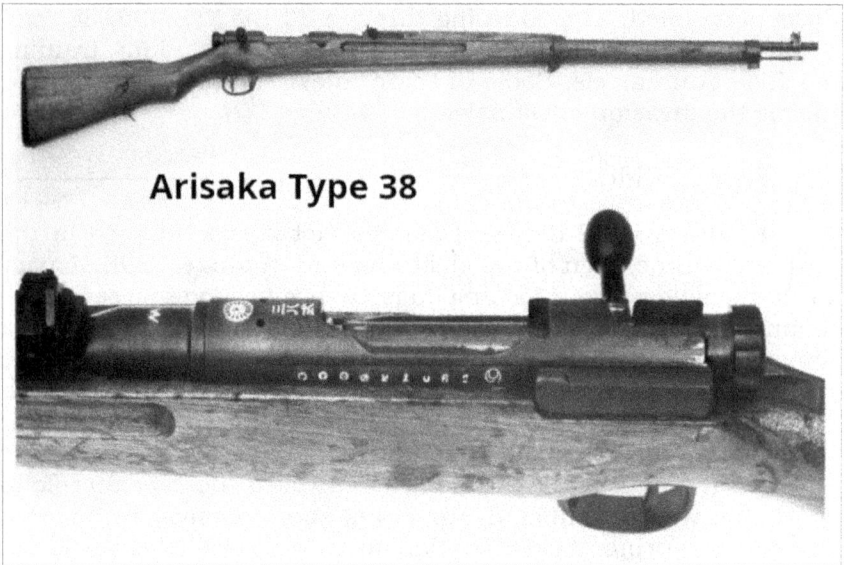

Arisaka Type 38

By 1940, three million plus Type 38s were built and issued to the Imperial Japanese Army. Its shortcomings during the Second Sino-Japanese War inspired the introduction of the new generation Type 99 rifle chambering the more potent 7.7×58mm Arisaka cartridge used by the Type 92 heavy machine gun and Type 97 light machine gun. However, not all units received the new rifle, and a mixture of incompatible cartridges led to significant logistical issues during World War II.

Description and Variant Types

The Type 38 rifle chambered the 6.5×50mm Arisaka cartridge, producing low recoil. However, its ballistic performance was on par with Norwegian and Italian-era 6.5mm military cartridges. That said, the 6.5×50mm was not as powerful as others in use by other nations. Also, there was scant spare room inside the

12

projectile for the tracer compound.

The Type 38, measuring 1,280 mm/50.4 inches overall, was the longest war rifle due. This was by design due to the Imperial Japanese Army's emphasis on bayonet training. The Japanese soldier of the era stood an average height was 160 centimeters/5 feet 3 inches short. His rifle was even longer when the 400 mm/15.75 inch long Type 30 bayonet was fixed. The Type 38 was heavy, weighing about 4.25 kg/9 pounds and six ounces.

Post-war inspection by the National Rifle Association and the US. Army's Aberdeen proving grounds concluded the Type 38 receiver was hands down the most robust bolt action of any of the world's nations and capable of chambering and firing significantly more powerful cartridges.

The Type 38 Carbine

The Type 38 carbine, intended for issue to engineers, quartermasters, the cavalry, and non-frontline troops, came into service concurrently with the Type 38 rifle. Its barrel measures 487 millimeters/19.2 inches long, with an overall length of 966 millimeters (38.0 in) and a weight of 3.3 kilograms (7.3 lb). The rifle lacked a bayonet. It was produced in several locations:
- Tokyo Arsenal, Japan, from 1906 until 1931, with an estimated 210,000 carbines built.
- Kokura arsenal from 1938 to 1941: 49,500 estimated built.
- Nagoya arsenal from 1935 to 1942: 206,000 estimated built.
- Hoten/Mukden arsenal from 1938 to 1944: 52,300 estimated built.

The Type 38 Cavalry Rifle

In the late 30s to early 40s, many Type 38 rifles were converted at Nagoya Arsenal into Cavalry Rifles. Nagoya previously rebuilt Type 38 and Type 44 rifles and carbines. Barrels were shortened to 635 mm/25.0 inches from the standard 794 mm/31.3 inches barrel, and the stock was trimmed to match the shortened barrel length while the hand guard retained its original size. The result: Type 38 is similarly-sized to the Type 99 Arisaka.

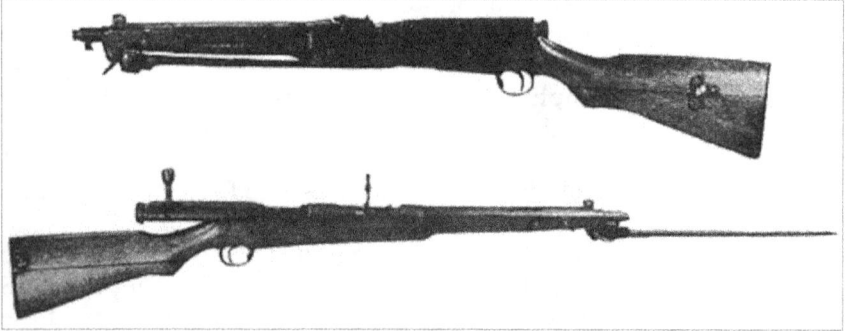

Its designation as a Cavalry Rifle is unusual in that, at that time, the cavalry branch was in decline. So naturally, it follows that it was far more likely these rifles were issued to second-line troops and not the cavalry. You might notice the lack of rhyme or reason to serial number sequences or arsenal markings. That's because the rifles were converted from existing inventory. While total production numbers are unknown, approximately 100,000 are estimated to have been converted.

The Type 44 Carbine

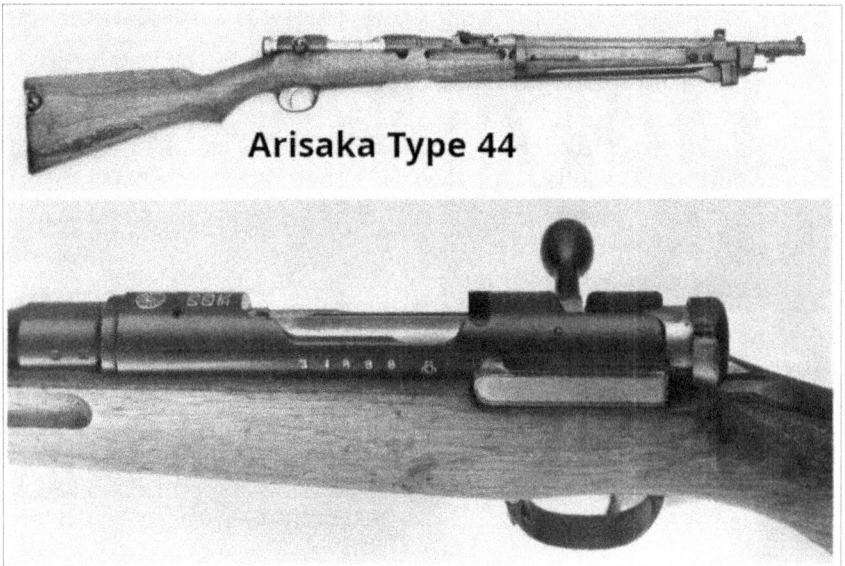

Arisaka Type 44

In 1911, the 44th year of Hirohito's reign, the Type 44 carbine was adopted. Following the standard Japanese calendar, rifles were designated by the adoption year's last one or two digits. Similar to the Type 38 Carbine from its middle band back, this cavalry carbine differs from the middle band forward. It features an under-folding bayonet, a metal nose cap, a stacking hook on the left side of the nose cap, and wide front sight guards. This model was introduced in 1911. There are three variations of this rifle. Each one is based entirely on the nose cap size and the spacing of the nose cap screws. They feature a butt stock storage compartment for a cleaning rod. Type 44 cavalry carbines were chambered in 6.5×50mm.

The Type 97 Sniper Rifle

The **Type 97 sniper rifle** (九七式狙撃銃, Kyū-nana-shiki sogekijū) was one of two main sniper rifles serving in Japan's Imperial military service. Evolved from the standard Type 38 and Type 97, they are fitted with a 2.5-magnification riflescope and a turned-down bolt handle necessary to clear the scope. Early models were equipped with a bipod. Like its progenitor, it too was chambered in the 6.5x50mm Arisaka cartridge. The internal 5-round box magazine is loaded either by a 5-round stripper clip or individual rounds.

As was the common practice on sniper rifles of the era, the optic was mounted offset, on the left of the receiver, to allow loading with stripper clips while allowing the sniper to employ

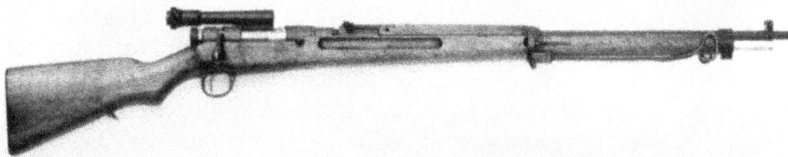

Type 97 Sniper Rifle

iron sights. Iron sights were a V-notched adjustable ladder graduated to 2200 meters. The scope mounts on a rail on the left side of the receiver, locking in place with a rotating locking lever. It dismounted easily. Issued with the rifle was a scope-carrying case, providing for dismounting and storage. The serial-numbered scope zeroed from the factory matched the rifle. The scope mount was designed to be removed easily and is mounted to the rifle's receiver using a rail with a rotating locking lever. Because the riflescope lacked elevation and windage adjustments, a mismatched scope and rifle would be out of zero.

The BDC-type reticle was calibrated for the 6.5X50 mm ballistics. Its vertical stadia lines range from 0- to 1500-meters, and horizontal stadia lines compensate for windage. The center of the crosshairs, where vertical and horizontal lines meet, is marked as 300 meters zero. The vertical line cants slightly to compensate for the scope's side mount.

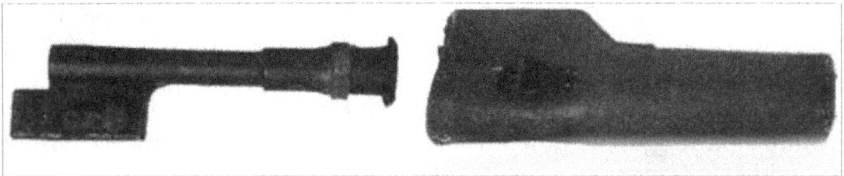

Scope and protective cover.

Type 97 was a large rifle. It is a long 31.4 inch/798 mm) barrel, an overall length of 50 inches/ 1.27 meters, weighing 8.6 pounds/3.9 kilograms. Due to its overly-long barrel, the rifle produced virtually no smoke or flash when fired, making it challenging to locate a sniper who had hidden and tied himself to the tops of trees or in other well-camouflaged positions.

Besides the standard 6.5X50 mm ammunition fielded by the Japanese during World War II, the Type 97 sniper rifle also fired a reduced charge cartridge in common with Type 11 and 96 light machine guns. Benefits included lighter recoil, reduced report, camouflaged muzzle flash, and better overall accuracy. Late-war production rifles were of poor quality and inaccurate. More than 20,000 sniper rifles were assembled at the Japanese Kokura and Nagoya arsenals from 1937 to 1945.

Model	Type 97 Sniper Rifle
Caliber	6.5x50mm Arisaka
Barrel Length	31.4-inches (798mm)
Weight	8.6-pounds (3.9 kg)
Length Overall	50-inches/1270mm

The Chinese Six/Five Infantry Rifle

The Chinese Six/Five infantry rifle is a copy of the Japanese Type 38. they were built in the late 1920s to early 1930 at the Taiyuan Arsenals for General Yen Hsi-sha, warlord of Shansi province. The receiver was marked as the Six/Five rifle in Chinese Kanji characters. An estimated 108,000 were made.

The Type 918 Rifle

These rifles are Type 38 copies, considered to have been built by the South Manchuria Army Arsenal, alternatively known as the 918 Arsenal. Very little is known about them. Chinese sources state type 918 rifles were made in China for Japan. Type 38s do not bear the Japanese Imperial Chrysanthemum. Instead, a heart symbol is roll-stamped on the receiver ring, and under it is written 918 Type. It is also unknown whether these weapons were built before or right after the surrender of Japanese forces. Its under-folding bayonet resembles the Japanese Type 44. The number 918 stamped on top of the receiver ring refers to the date of the Mukden Incident, September 18, 1931.

The North China Type 19 Carbine

This crude copy of the Type 38 carbine is believed to have been manufactured primarily in Tientsin, China. Likely intended for puppet troops, and unlike the other Type 19, it faithfully copies the Type 30 carbine's working parts but is chambered in caliber 7.92×57mm Mauser.

This particular Type 19 variant chambered in the Japanese 6.5x50sr caliber shows a cherry blossom roll stamped on its receiver instead of the Japanese Imperial Chrysanthemum. Further, it is marked North China Type 19.

The number 19 is believed to mean the 19th year of the Showa Era or 1944. Its proper nomenclature remains unknown. Approximately 40,000 carbines were produced. During WW2, Thailand was a co-belligerent of Japan and was given 6.5mm Arisaka rifles and carbines.

In 1924, Siam, now known as the Kingdom of Thailand, ordered 50,000 Type 38 rifles from the Tokyo Army Arsenal chambered in Type 66 8x52R caliber. The Siamese Chakra, a spinning, celestial discus with 108 serrated edges, marks the receiver with Type 66 written beneath.

The Siamese Type 66 Long Rifle

In 1924 Siam, now known as the Kingdom of Thailand, ordered 50,000 Type 38 rifles from Tokyo Army Arsenal. Chambered in Type 66, 8x52R caliber, the receiver is stamped with the Siamese Chakra with Type 66 inscribed below. Not only was the caliber altered, but the sights, bayonet, and cleaning rod differed from their Japanese counterpart—virtually none of the parts, including screws, interchange with the Japanese Type 38.

When the firearm was adopted, the eight-bladed Sudarshana Chakra accompanied the word Type (แบบ) with the last two numbers of the Thai Buddhist Era calendar.

Thailand, formerly known as Siam, remained independent while all the other nations fell to colonial rule. The Thai crest is the Chakra, a disk with sharpened cutting blades around its circumference, is found in several variations of design in its center. Two distinct Sudarshana Chakra receiver crests emblazoned on the receiver represented the mythological flaming throwing weapon used by the Hindu God Vishnu. This actual Siamese /Thai Type 2466 rifle was not based on the Mauser action but instead the Japanese Type 38. They were called: ปืนเล็ก ยาว แบบ ๒๔๖๖; Bpeun Lék Yaao Bàep Sŏng Pan Sèe Rói Hòk Sìp Hòk; Small Arms Long Rifle Type 2466, all chambered in caliber 8 x 52R mm Type 2466.

In 1923 Thailand placed a contract for 50,000 of these rifles with the Japanese Pacific Union (Taihei Kumiai) export firm. Said rifles were to be built by the Imperial Japanese Army Weapons Arsenal, Tokyo Arsenal (陸軍造兵廠 東京工廠), located in the Koishikawa District of Tokyo, Japan, from 1924 to 1928. These rifles were shipped to Thailand in four separate batches from 1924 to 1928.

Not only had the caliber been changed, but the sights, bayonet, and cleaning rod were also different than the Japanese version. Almost all parts, including screws, do not interchange with the Japanese Type 38.

An improvement over the Type 30 Arisaka, Type 35 was developed for the Imperial Japanese Navy Special Naval Landing Forces issue. Notably, it was the first Arisaka with a dust cover. First completed in 1902, the Type 35 started being phased out for the Type 38 sometime around 1905. Blade front and 2,000-yard tangent rear sights, with a solid chrysanthemum and Type nomenclature on the receiver ring, the Tokyo Arsenal stamp, serial number, and a small "sun wheel" on the rear bridge. The sun wheel crest of Siam (aka Thailand) suggests a military contract sale either during the original production period or after Type 35 had been phased out of Japanese service. The dust cover is sheet metal with a spring-loaded retaining clip. When the dust cover opens for firing, a set of vent holes line up with matching holes in the chamber. On the underside of its pistol grip, the multi-piece butt stock, replete with sling swivels and a flat butt plate, displays a small Japanese naval arsenal stamp.

From 1899 to around 1905, with the introduction of Type 38, Type 30 was the standard infantry rifle of Imperial Japan. This rifle features an inverted V-blade front sight and a V-notch rear sight. Mounted on a folding ladder, the leaf graduated to 1,900 yards with a 2,000-yard topmost notch. The un-serialized receiver features an Imperial mum stamp and Type 30 markings. The sliding dust cover is manually operated. A small, spiral floral symbol, which appears to be the crest of Siam at the rear receiver bridge, indicates a sale or exchange from military surplus after Type 38 introduction. The pistol grip stock is smooth with a flat steel butt plate.

19

The Thai Type 83 Rifle

Unlike the Siamese Type 66, the Type 83 rifle is a standard Japanese Type 38 chambered in 6.5x50sr sent as aid from Japan to Thailand in 1940. These went straight from the Nagoya and Kokura Arsenals loading docks to Thailand, but only after obliterating the Japanese Imperial Chrysanthemum by stamping a circle of zeros around the periphery of the petals. During the Franco-Thai War, Thailand issued these rifles to second-line troops, freeing rifles in their main caliber from front-line duties. Late in the 1950s, some weapons barrels and stocks were shortened. Many were re-chambered for .30-06 Type 88 cartridges, becoming Type 83/88s. Because terms of the Gun Control Act of 1968 restricted military arms from entering the country, very few were imported into the United States

Thai Type 91 Police Carbines

Made at the Royal Thai Arsenal, Bangkok, these WWII-era **Type 91 Police Carbines** were assembled from a Type 38 parts bin, making a carbine for police. Stock and barrel were shortened. Rifle stocks were inletted to attach M1 carbine slings and oilers. Some bolts were turned down. Others were left intact. The Royal Thai police symbol and the number 91 were stamped on some receivers. Others received the Siamese Chakra. All retained the original Japanese 6.5x50sr caliber chambering.

Mexican Model 1913 Rifles and Carbines

In mid-1913, Mexico's Huerta Government ordered 50,000 rifles and 25,000 carbines from the Tokyo Artillery Arsenal compatible with Mexican Mauser model 1895, 1902, or 1910 bayonets. The first 10,000-15,000 rifles arrived in Mexico in early 1914. Then Huerta went into exile. Japan, fearing nonpayment for the balance of the weapons shipment, summarily canceled the order.

In late 1914, Imperial Russia, desperate for firearms, bought the remainder of 35,400 or 60,000 orphaned rifles and carbines abandoned in Japan. The first few thousand rifles displayed three interlocking circles stamped on the receiver. The rest had a Mexican crest under the words proclaiming: Republica Mexicana.

Estonian converted standard Type 38s to the .303 British cartridge. Intended for issue to Estonian Defence League second-line troops, 24,000 rifles were re-chambered during 1929-1934.

Mexican Model 1913 Rifles and Carbines Users

- Burma: Burmese fighters used abandoned/captured weapons against the Japanese.
- The National Revolutionary Army: During the Second Sino-Japanese War, rifles captured from and used against Japanese forces
- PLA People's Liberation Army, Captured from and used against Japanese forces.
- Estonia: Ex-Russian stock used in the Estonian War of Independence. 24,000 Type 38s were converted to .303 British.
- Finland: Ex-Russian stock
- France: Purchased during World War I
- Indonesia: After Japan's surrender in WWII, her captured weapons were put to good use in the Indonesian War of Independence.
- Empire of Japan
- Manchukuo
- Malaysia: Captured after Japan's World War II surrendered, then carried into battle by the Malaysian Communist Party in the Malayan Emergency.
- Mexico: In 1913, the Mexican government ordered 75,000 rifles and carbines in 7×57mm Mauser. Ultimately, only about 10,000 to 15,000 were delivered before President Victoriano Huerta's exile in 1914, causing Japan to wisely suspend the order.
- Second Polish Republic: Ex-Russian stock
- Russian Empire: During World War I, Russia bought 35,400 orphaned rifles initially intended for Mexico. It received 128,000 Type 30 and 38 rifles from Britain in

1916. In addition, Russia ordered 600,000 6.5 mm weapons directly from Japan.

• Thailand: Before World War I, Thailand bought rifles from Japan

• The United Kingdom bought 150,000 Type 30 and 38s from Japan at the beginning of World War I. Most of them served with training battalions. Britain declared them obsolete in 1921. Japanese exports of this model were much more significant: 500,000 went to Great Britain, and another 620,000 to Russia.

• Vietnam: During the war with France, Viet Minh irregulars used rifles that Japanese occupation troops had abandoned in Indochina. Think jungle trails and the French defeat at Dien Bien Phu.

The Type 99

Arisaka Type 99

Type 99 was the successor to the Type 38 rifle. Chambered in 7.7×58mm Type 99. Later rimless variants of Type 92 and 97 cartridges are also usable.

During World War I, Imperial Japanese troops carried 6.5 mm bolt-action Arisakas. Early in the 1930s, during the Second Sino-

22

Japanese War, Japan's military minds noticed the 7.7mm cartridge fired by its Type 92 heavy machine guns in China had better stopping power than Type 38's 6.5×50mm cartridge. Long story made short, Tokyo wanted a more powerful weapon to replace the outclassed Type 38.

The Imperial Japanese Army developed a rifle based evolved from the Type 38 rifle but with a more potent 7.7mm caliber. Type 99s were built at nine different arsenals., Seven arsenals were located in Japan. Two others were located offshore—one in Mukden, China the other in Jinsen, Korea.

The standard rifle featured a wire monopod and an antiaircraft fixture mounted on the rear sight. Type 99 qualifies as the first mass-produced infantry rifle with a chrome-lined bore, a feature that eased cleaning and minimized corrosion from corrosive-primed ammunition. By mid-war, all three features were abandoned.

Designed in 1939 and produced and fielded from 1941 to 1945, Type 99 was hands down the most ubiquitous Imperial Japanese service rifle of World War II. Further, with 2,500,000 built, it was the second-most produced Imperial rifle. Significant upgrades from the type 38 include transitioning the rear sight from a Type 38 V-notch type to an aperture. The front sight blade profile was reconfigured to a triangular shape. Barrels were chrome-plated. In early production, the rear sight was equipped with fold-out antiaircraft sighting arms.

Sub-variations include a long rifle (approximately only 38,000 made) and a short rifle. The former measured 1258 mm/49.5 inches in total length, and the latter 1118 mm/46.7 inches. The short rifle varied in build quality from initial to intermediate and ultimately to the bottom of the barrel, last-ditch. Type 99 Short rifles built after mid-war (also known as the Type 99, last-ditch) have neither a flip-up antiaircraft rear sight nor a monopod.

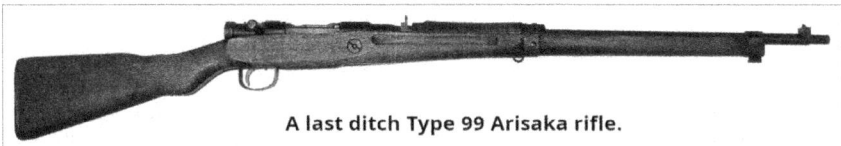
A last ditch Type 99 Arisaka rifle.

The ambitious intention was to, by the end of the war, completely replace the outdated Type 38 with the new and improved Type 99. However, the war in the Pacific Theater of

Operation's logistical demands prevented the Japanese army from completely replacing the Type 38. The Imperial Japanese military fielded both rifles during the conflict. As the war progressed, from Pacific island to island, cost-saving steps to speed up production came online. Due to their crudeness in finishing the late war, rifles became known as the Last Ditch or Substitute Standard. In comparison, they are generally as crude as 1945- dated Mauser K98ks of Germany, or worse. Type 99s were built in four versions during their service life:

- ✔ Type 99 regular issue.
- ✔ Type 99 short rifle.
- ✔ Type 99 long rifle.
- ✔ Type 2 Paratroop Rifle (Take-down model).
- ✔ Type 99 Sniper Rifle.

Other Type 99 Users

Under American supervision at the Tokyo arsenal during the Korean War, 6,650 long and 126,500 short type 99s were modified to chamber the .30-06 Springfield cartridge. Ostensibly intended for issue to South Korean *gendarmerie*, by the cease-fire in 1953, few rifles appear to have been issued. U.S. Type 99s received a lengthened magazine well. A small notch cut in the top aft of the receiver ring made room for the tip of the .30-06 Springfield round, measuring a 1/3 inch longer. No big surprise, accuracy suffered due to the difference in rifling rate of twist, but they were nonetheless functional. Civilians have also performed conversions to both .30-06 and 7.62mm NATO, often along with sporterizing modifications to the stock.

After 1946, the People's Republic of China re-chambered large numbers of its Type 99 rifles to chamber the 8×57 I.S. cartridge.

During the Indonesian National Revolution, Indonesian troops fielded many Type 99 rifles in their fight against the Dutch(1945–1949).

After 1945, the Royal Thai Army received all manner and sorts of Japanese rifles and re-chambering many Type 99 short rifles to fire the U.S. .30-06 Springfield cartridge.

To benefit from the superior stopping power of the 7.7mm cartridge, several caliber 6.5mm Type 38 rifles were modified. Although tests proved satisfactory, the army decided against adding the more substantial recoil and larger chamber dimensions of the 7.7mm cartridge compared to the Type 38. Instead, they surmised converting to 7.7mm would require an entirely new rifle. This is despite Type 99's increased recoil due to its lighter weight combined with a heavier cartridge.

Its cock-on-closing action improved the rate of fire compared to the Mauser cock-on-open design. The rifle's unique safety mechanism operates by pressing in on a knurled disk at the back of the bolt with the palm and rotating it 1/8 clockwise turn.

It had the standard quick-release bolt and antiaircraft sights, a sliding bolt cover, and a monopod. The bolt cover, while well-intentioned, proved highly problematic. Many soldiers simply discarded them due to their excessive rattling that defeated noise discipline while on patrol.

Type 99 was an excellent weapon. Still, as with all bolt guns fielded during World War II, they were outclassed in close combat by semi-automatic rifles and submachine guns.

Type 99 is one of the most robust military bolt rifles ever made. That said, many late-war (last ditch) rifles used lower quality parts, a complete lack of finish, and shortcuts were taken to ease production. Rough machining marks on the metal easily distinguish last-ditch rifles, along with a poorly finished stock, a wooden butt plate, a fixed rear sight, and an unfinished cocking piece and bolt handle. Such late-war rifles should be considered unsafe to fire.

In some cases, these rifles may have been training rifles intended for firing blank cartridges. Training rifle receivers and barrels were machined from mild steel and are inappropriate for the high chamber pressures of ball ammunition. Aficionados suggest accounts of Type 99 rifles blowing were the results of soldiers testing-firing captured drill rifles, mistakenly firing ball ammunition with tragic consequences. Perhaps such a scenario led to Arisakas being branded with a reputation for poor construction.

The Type 99's bayonet's long, slender blade was grooved to reduce weight. Early models featured a hooked *quillion*. These bayonets were attached to a lug under the barrel, stabilized by a loop around the muzzle. Unmounted, it was handheld and wielded like a machete or a short sword.

Type 99 Variants

Type 99 long rifles were built at Nagoya and Toyo Kogyounder.

Kokura Arsenal supervision. Like early Type 99s, these Type 99 long rifles featured a monopod. Antiaircraft lead arms on the rear sight and the ubiquitous dust cover. Between the summer of 1940 and the spring of 1941, 38,000 were built: 8,000 at Nagoya and another 30,000 at Toyo Kogyo. Then production switched to the Type 99 short rifle. Millions were made.

Type 99 Availability

While Arisaka rifles have never been imported to the USA in great numbers, thousands upon thousands were brought home by sailors, soldiers, and marines returning from the Pacific Theater of Operations. Under General Douglas MacArthur's orders, the Imperial Chrysanthemum adorning the top of the receiver was supposed to be defaced. Not all were. The mark certified the rifle was the Emperor's personal property. Defacing preserved the Emperor's honor.

Rifles with their chrysanthemum intact bring a premium price to the collector's market. A price sometimes doubles that of a defaced rifle. Due to the scarcity of factory 7.7×58mm Arisaka ammunition, many rifles have been re-chambered to standard calibers over the years. Because of its robust action, like other rifles of the period, it is particularly suitable for conversion.

Type 99 Users

- Flag of the National Revolutionary Army National Revolutionary Army: re-chambered for the 8×57mm I.S. cartridge after 1946
- PLA Chinese Red Army
- Indonesia: used during the Indonesian National Revolution
- Empire of Japan
- Malaysia: captured during World War II and used by the Malayan Races Liberation Army of Malayan Communist Party during the Malayan Emergency
- North Korea: used during the Korean War

- The Philippines captured limited numbers of Arisakas during World War II, which Filipino and American guerrillas fighters subsequently fielded.
- South Korea: Many were converted to .30-06, but few were ever issued
- Thailand: used after 1945, in the early 1950s, some converted to the .30-06 cartridge

Type 99 Sniper Rifle

The Type 99, used during the Second World War, was a sniper version of the Type 99 rifle. Chambered in the 7.7×58mm round, there were a few variations. Some featured a straight bolt and riflescope mounted on the left side of the receiver, which allowed loading cartridges via stripper clips. Another variation had a bent bolt and the scope above the receiver, which required the sniper dangling in a tree top clumsily load rounds one at a time. The T99's shorter barrel, combined with a larger caliber round, made concealment more complicated than it had with the Type 97 sniper rifle that preceded it, considering the louder muzzle blast and flash caused by the increased powder capacity.

The Imperial Japanese Military's other sniper rifle was built on long and short model T99s, the latter being more numerous. Chambered in 7.7×58mm, the larger, heavier projectile, pushed by a heftier powder charge, meant a bullet less affected by windage, albeit at the cost of a more substantial recoil.

Sniper rifles were issued with one of two different types of scopes: the Type 97 2.5X and the Type 99 4-power telescopic sight. Later, iterations of riflescope boasted range settings. Each scope was issued with a holster for safekeeping the riflescope while it was detached from the rifle. By doctrine, snipers were selected by their marksmanship prowess. Production began in May 1942. The total number made is approximately 10,000.

TERA Rifle

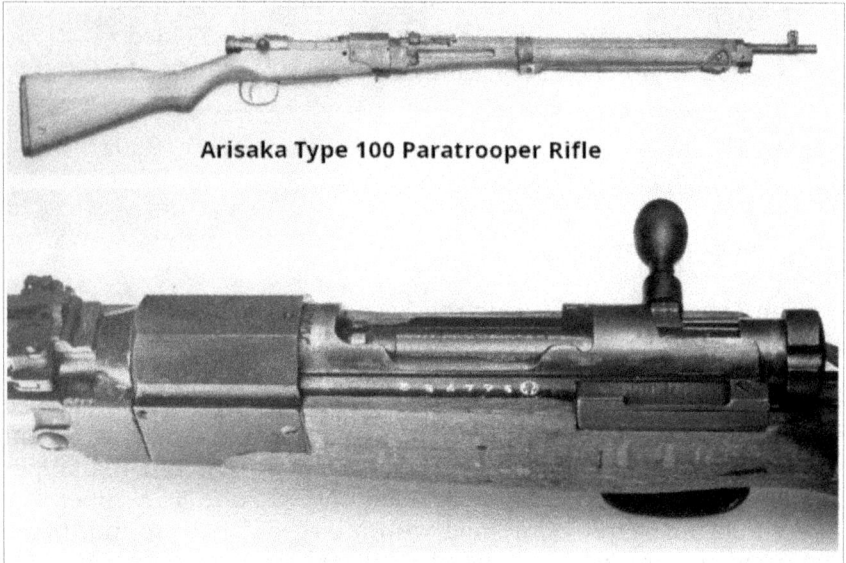

Arisaka Type 100 Paratrooper Rifle

The TERA Rifles (Teishin Rakkasan Shyoujyu), developed for paratroopers of the Imperial Japanese Army, broke down or folded into two parts. Easily disassembled or assembled, there was a single production model with two prototypes: Type 100, based on the Karabiner 98k Fallschirmjäger detachable-barrel *Abnehmbarer Lauf* variant, never went into production because its folding mechanism proved unreliable.

Type 1 was based on the Type 38 cavalry rifle and faithfully replicated the take-apart mechanism of the Karabiner 98k Klappschaft. It did not separate but instead folded.

Founded on the Type 99 Rifle, the Type 2 broke down into two parts: stock and action and barrel and sights. In the Clint Eastwood film Dirty Harry, Type 2 gained Hollywood notoriety as the sniper rifle used by the Scorpio killer.

A limited production run of take-down rifles was built for the Imperial army and navy paratroopers. The single production model fielded, Type 2, was based on the Type 99 short rifle. The other two were prototypes, particularly Type 100 and Type 1. Type 100, alternately known as Type 0, was one of Japan's first experiments in paratroop rifles. Manufactured from standard Nagoya Arsenal Type 99 rifles, Type 100's interrupted lugs at the chamber allowed the rifle to separate into two sections. Only a few hundred were manufactured. Ultimately the Type 2 design with its locking wedge was adopted.

Type 2 is chambered in 7.7×58mm Type 99. Later rimless variants of Type 92 and 97 cartridges were also in use. Type 2 allowed for compact storage, breaking down into two components: the stock and action and barrel and hand guard. About a total of 19,000 were built from 1942 to 1944.

BAYONETS

Worthy of note, it has been claimed that the Japanese soldier logged more than 200-hours of bayonet training, compared to the U.S. Soldier's ten or twenty. Created concurrently with the Type 30 rifle, the type 30 sword-type bayonet fits over the muzzle of all Arisaka variants except the Type 44 carbine. Twenty variations exist, subcategorized by early, mid, and late-war production phases. Besides Arisak rifles, Type 30s also fit Type 96 and 99 light machine guns.

The Type 30 Bayonet

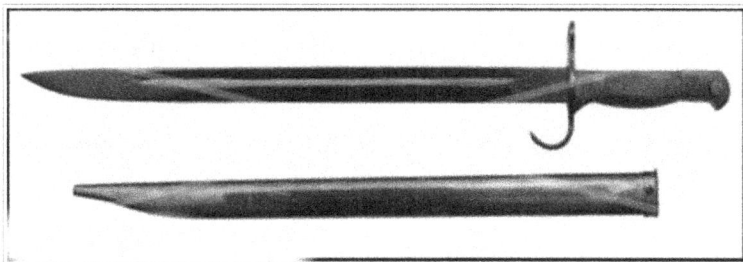

The Type 30 Bayonet is a single-edged sword bayonet with a 400-millimeter/15.75-inch blade, weighing 700 grams/1.5 pounds, and an overall length of 514 millimeters/20.24 inches. Alternatively, it is known as the Pattern 1897 bayonet. Early Type 30 bayonets sported a distinctive hooked quillion intended to hook and break an opposing soldier's bayonet. In combat, they proved ineffective. By 1942 the quillon was deleted to save materials and decrease production time, leaving a straight, hand guard. The length of the blade provided the average Japanese infantryman with sufficient reach to pierce the abdomen of an enemy cavalryman. The blades suffered several maladies caused by poor quality forging, tending to rust quickly, lose their edge, and break when bent. The bayonets were manufactured from 1897 to 1945 at Kokura Arsenal, Koishikawa Arsenal (Tokyo), and Nagoya Arsenal and were under contract by Toyoda Automatic Loom, Matsushita, and others.

Type 35 Bayonet

Type 35 was a slightly modified Type 30 bayonet explicitly made for the Type 35 rifle. The dimensions of the bayonet are nearly identical to the Type 30 bayonet. The difference between the two is a spring catch that hooks into the scabbard, holding it secure when not used. About 8,400,000 were made.

Type 44 Spike Bayonet

Fixed permanently on Type 44 carbines, the Type 44 spike-type bayonet folds under the hand guard so as not to interfere with the barrel when deployed.

Type 2 Bayonet

The extreme length of the Type 30 bayonet rendered it unfit for concealing within a paratrooper's kit. Type 2' shorter knife- blade-like bayonet addressed the issue. Its dimensions: Twenty centimeters/7.8 inches shorter than a Type 30, and its total length measures 32.3 cm/12.9 inches. Primarily paired with a Type 2 TERA rifle or the Type 100 submachine gun by the Imperial Military Airborne Divisions, about 25,000 were made.

Final Notes

In the real world, captured foreign firearms can be dangerous to shoot due to the lower quality of last-ditch rifles produced during the final days of World War II. Also potentially dangerous: Mismatched bolts and modifications performed on said rifles by returning U.S. service members.

Initially, Arisaka ammunition was a battlefield pick-up, not readily available after the war's end. Consequently, many Arisaka were re-chambered to available calibers of that time. Additionally, some were rendered inoperable before being shipped home. Arisakas were demilitarized by permanently damaging the receiver or outright removal of critical parts.

Type 38s were commonly re-chambered to the 6.5×.257 Roberts wildcat cartridge, formed by modifying .257 Roberts cases with its neck expanded to fit 6.5mm bullets.

Similarly, Type 99s (caliber 7.7×58mm) were commonly converted to .30-06 Springfield, similar but not quite identical dimensions. Caliber .30-06 ammunition can be fired in type 99s by lengthening the chamber from 58 to 63mm. The broader dimensioned 7.7mm case also uses a somewhat larger-diameter bullet. So naturally, it follows a fired .30-06 cartridge case swells to fit the oversized dimensions of the Japanese chamber. A .308 diameter/ .30-06 bullet fits loosely in Type 99's wider .310-312 diameter rifling. As a result, accuracy suffers.

American civilian shooters seeking ammunition for Type 99 rifles improvise rounds by modifying fired and virgin .30-06 cases. Pulled German 7.92×57mm Mauser and British .303 .311 bullets fit the Arisaka rifling.

The 7.7x58 mm chamber is slightly larger in diameter than the .30-06 Springfield cartridge case. When fired in an Arisaka chamber, .30-06 reformed brass bulges a mite. As a result, some savvy shooters prefer using the correct brass or new factory cartridges. Military surplus .303 British bullets and powder charges loaded in 7.7×58mm cases produce ballistics similar to the original Japanese military load.

As for newly minted ammunition, Sweden's Norma manufactures 7.7×58mm ammunition and unprimed brass cases for reloaders. Hornady loads Arisaka ammunition in both 6.5mm and 7.7mm calibers.

During World War II, **Nagoya Arsenal,** a rambling collection of five major military facilities, produced the Arisaka Type 99 rifle. Specific arsenal facilities in Atsuta, Chikusa, Takagi, and Toriimatsu.

After the war, **Torimatsu,** responsible for producing Type 99 rifles, was converted to a paper plant (Ouji Seshi) in Kasugai. Today, travel to the site on the Japan Railways Group Chūō Main Line from Nagoya, several stops northeast of Chikusa station. Throughout the Second World War, Toyo Kogyo produced weapons for the Japanese military, most notably the series 30 through 35 Type 99 rifles.

Established in 1916, the Kokura Arms Factory (小倉兵器製造所 Kokura Heiki Seizōjo), one of six arsenals under government control arsenal, manufactured various machine guns, cannons, and rifles. The others were Tokyo Arsenal, Nizō Arsenal (second Tokyo Arsenal), Nagoya Arsenal, Osaka Arsenal, and the South Manchurian Arsenal.

The **Kokura Military Arsenal** Kokura, Kyushu, Japan(小倉陸軍造兵廠 Kokura Rikugun Zōheishō), commonly known as the Kokura Arsenal (小倉工廠 Kokura Kōshō), a Japanese state owned-arsenal active from (1916 to 1945) produced many of Japan's small arms, including:

Arisaka - bolt-action rifles
Type 100 submachine gun - submachine guns
Type 96 light machine gun - light machine guns
Type 99 light machine gun - light machine gun

Kokura, one of Japan's largest munitions plants, is notable for having been the primary target for the Fat Man atomic warhead dropped by the U.S. Army Air Force on August 9, 1945. The morning of the air raid, the city, obscured by morning fog, was mistaken for the neighboring town of Yahata. Mission commander Major Charles Sweeney ordered to drop his bomb visually, not by radar, and diverted his B-29 Superfortress bomber, *Bockscar*, to the secondary target, Nagasaki.

After the war ended, InterArmco and other purveyors of military surplus bolt guns imported boatloads of Lee-Enfields, M1917 Enfields, Mausers, 03 and 03A3 Springfields, and Japanese Arisakas to the United States. Noted firearms writer P.O. Ackley wondered which ones were safe for hand loads. He tested all of them. Destructive tests proved the Type 99 Arisaka action to be the most robust. In short, he tried to blow up a Type 99 Arisaka and failed!

At the Aberdeen Proving Grounds, General Julian S. Hatcher, Army Ordnance Corps, repeated the experiment and confirmed the results. His lab further revealed that Type 99 bolts and receivers were machined from an alloy similar to SAE steel grade 1085, boasting a carbon content of 0.80% to 0.90% and manganese content of 0.60% to 0.90%. Very late war, Arisaka rifles were founded upon poor-quality steel.

Hatcher's notes also point out how the Arisaka chamber completely surrounds the cartridge within the barrel shank and boasts excellent gas venting in the event of a ruptured case.

Military surplus Arisakas exported to the United States include Type 38 carbines re-barrelled and re-chambered to caliber

7.62×39mm Russian. Some Type 38 rifles captured by the Chinese Kuomintang forces were converted to fire the 7.92×57mm Mauser round. In 1910, a minimal run of Type 38 rifles was manufactured for export to the Republic of Mexico, proudly emblazoned with the Mexican coat of arms in place of the Imperial Chrysanthemum. Few of the rifles arrived before the Mexican Revolution. Most of these rifles remained in Japan until World War One until sold to weapons-hungry Imperial Russia.

Japanese Rifle Manufacturers and Their Symbols

Symbol	Arsenal/ Subcontractor	Period of Operation
	Koishikawa Arsenal (Tokyo)	1870-1935
	Kokura Arsenal	1935-1945
	Nagoya Arsenal	1923-1945
	Jinsen Arsenal (Korea)	1923-1945
	Mukden Arsenal (Manchuria)	1931-1945
	Toyo Kogyo	1939-1945
	Tokyo Juki Kogyo	1940-1945
	Tokyo Juki Kogyo	1940-1945
	Howa Jyuko	1940-1945
	Izawa Jyuko	1940-1945

Kokura Arsenal proofmark used at Tokyo Arsenal prior to 1935.

Japanese Rifle Production Figures

Type	Arsenal/ Subcontractor	Series	Serial number range	Dates
38	Koishikawa (Tokyo)	none	0-2,029,000	1906-ca.1935
	Kokura	20	29,000-49,000	1933-1940
		22	0-99,999	
		23	0-99,999	
		24	0-99,999	
		25	0-99,999	
		26	0-71,000	
	Nagoya	none	2,021,000-2,031,000	1923-ca.1933
		26	0-99,999	ca.1933-ca.1940
		27	0-99,999	
		28	0-99,999	
		29	0-8,000	
	Jinsen (Korea)	none	0-1,400	ca.1939-ca.1940
		30	1,000-13,000	
	Mukden (Manchuria)	none	0-30,000	ca.1934-ca.1940
		none	5,000,000-5,065,000	
		none	65,000-79,000	
38 Concentric Circle	Nagoya	none	0-2,600	??
	Kokura	none	0-1,500	??
38 Carbine	Koishikawa (Tokyo)	none	0-212,000	1906-ca.1935
	Kokura	2	12,000-92,000	ca.1933-ca.1940
	Nagoya	none	0-2,000	1923-ca.1933
		4	0-99,999	ca.193

35

				3-ca.1940
		5	0-99,999	
		6	0-4,000	
	Mukden (Manchuria)	none	0-7,000	ca.193 4-ca.1940
		none	600,000- 628,000	
		6	29,000- 44,000	
44	Koishikawa (Tokyo)	none	0-56,000	1911- ca.1933
	Kokura	none	56,000- 70,000	ca.193 3-ca.1940
		1	0-9,000	
	Nagoya	none	0-2,000	ca.193 0-ca.1933
		2	0-12,000	ca.193 3-ca.1940
99	Nagoya	none	0-99,999	1939- 1945
		1	0-99,999	
		2	2,500-99,999	
		3	0-99,999	
		4	10,000- 99,999	
		5	0-99,999	
		6	0-99,999	
		7	0-99,999	
		8	0-99,999	
		10	0-99,999	
		11	0-99,999	
		12	0-1,000	
	Kokura	20	0-99,999	1939- 1945
		21	0-99,999	
		22	0-99,999	
		23	0-99,999	
		24	0-99,999	
		25	0-92,000	
	Toyo Kogyo	30	0-99,999	1939- 1945
		31	0-99,999	

		32	0-99,999	
		33	0-99,999	
		34	0-99,999	
		35	0-57,000	
	Tokyo Juki Kogyo	27	0-41,000	1940-1945
		37	0-59,000	
	Izawa Jyuko	4	0-10,000	1940-1945
		9	0-50,000	
	Howa Jyuko	9	50,000-99,999	1940-1945
	Jinsen Arsenal	40	0-91,000	1939-1945
	Mukden Arsenal	45	0-3,000	1939-1945
99 Concentric Circle	Nagoya	none	0-600	
	Nagoya	none	none (assembly numbers 0-700)	
	Tokyo Juki Kogyo	2	0-600	
	Kokura	none	0-1,400	
	Kokura	none	1,800-3,400	

37

www.ingramcontent.com/pod-product-compliance
Lightning Source LLC
Chambersburg PA
CBHW071752020426
42331CB00008B/2282